MW00355352

"This journal workbook could be one of the most important books you'll ever hold, because it will also hold you. Robyn's words, unobtrusive thoughts and beautiful life giving wisdom will be like a midwife for you, if you are anything like me, helping you gently bring forth your own truth, and being, and self. Take my advice—and a long deep breath—and begin the journey of a lifetime."

Anne Lamott, *New York Times* bestselling author of
Stitches, Bird by Bird, Traveling Mercies and many others

"Robyn's tender and soul nourishing wisdom weaves throughout and you will feel guided and supported to explore and discover all that you are and what you feel. Going inward with this book will lead you to develop even more exquisite self-care, self-acceptance and self-LOVE."

SARK, author and artist of *Succulent Wild Woman*,
Transformation Soup, and many others

"Robyn's wise and thoughtful words on the pages of this journal invite you to write your way to a deeper acceptance of yourself. Each page will take you to your core. Exploring the possibilities that Robyn offers here will help you to hear and embrace all of your self. This book could become your best friend."

Myrna Fleishman, Ph.D., Psychotherapist and artist,
Santa Barbara, CA

"This journal is an exceptional tool to use for self-exploration. The quotes on the edge of each page are ideal for taking a simple idea and finding ways to apply it to our own lives. There is a love that comes through the pages that encourages you to take the time to be with yourself. It is gift that you give to yourself each time you sit down with the journal and write."

Dr. Caitlin J. Matthews, Chiropractor, Ojai, CA

"This unique journal, with its generous space and nuggets of inspiring wisdom, encourages you to write, doodle, draw, scribble...whatever furthers your personal journey. No recipes here—just room to be the authentic you, in the company of Robyn's wise soul."

Vivian Sudhalter, Professional Wordsmith/Editor, Ojai, CA

"There are so many motivational types of workbooks, encouraging us to get more done, to be more, to have more. But I've found that doing or having more of the things that didn't work to begin with never gave me peace or contentment. It just made me feel like I was never going to be 'good' enough. With Robyn's wisdom and encouragement, I've learned that doing less, letting my belly feelings lead the way, I am able to find joy and peace in just having my own deep self love, protection and care."

Julie A. Levin, MFT, Marriage & Family Therapist, Pleasant Hill, CA

What reviewers have written about: Robyn's first book
Go Only as Fast as Your Slowest Part Feels Safe to Go:
Tales to Kindle Gentleness and Compassion for Our Exhausted Selves

"The material and stories in this book are beautiful and riveting, rich in wisdom and compassion, at once healing and exciting. I think this book will fill you with the hope of having the life you were born to live and the life you've dreamed of, because this book is about our souls and hearts; about peace, gladness, and freedom."

Anne Lamott, *New York Times* bestselling author of *Stitches, Traveling Mercies, Bird by Bird,* and many others

"If your inner critic has been working overtime, if other people's opinions are more important to you than your own, if you would like to learn how to soothe yourself in times of stress and distress, pick up this book."

Nicole S. Urdang, M.S., NCC, DHM, LMHC, Holistic Psychotherapist, Buffalo, N.Y.

"If you have ever wondered how self-acceptance looks, sounds and feels, this book is for you. If replacing self-reproach with self-nurturing seems like a good idea, but you haven't got a clue, this book is a must read.

Robyn's work is invaluable in learning to develop the warm, soothing, internal presence necessary to sit in the middle of your feelings/your life. An extraordinary gift from an extraordinarily gifted and courageous guide!"

Carol H. Munter, co-author, *Overcoming Overeating* and *When Women Stop Hating Their Bodies*

"If you've been wanting the guidebook through the land of your truest self, you will LOVE, LOVE, LOVE this book!"

Julie A. Levin, MFT, Marriage & Family Therapist, Pleasant Hill, CA

"When I first received Robyn's book I knew it was a sacred book – I call it the Bible. It is an incredible gift she has given to the world that reminds us to be kind and compassionate with ourselves. The thoughts in her book are deep truths that our bodies and souls know to be true. There is a quiet peace that you can feel when you read her book."

Dr. Caitlin J. Matthews, Chiropractor, Ojai, CA

What reviewers have written about: Robyn's third book
Choosing Gentleness: Opening Our Hearts to All the
Ways We Feel and Are in Every Moment

"This is a heart-singing book, filled with wisdom, tenderness, joy and humor about our soul and spirit, and the child inside. *Choosing Gentleness* is poetry and essays and artwork about healing, about accepting and even celebrating every aspect of our true beings, even the scary parts—yikes! Rich in truth and revelation and instruction, it is a song to the Self and it is a delightful way home, in the company of a singing, dancing woman of depth and quirk and general amazing ways."

Anne Lamott, *New York Times* bestselling author of *Traveling Mercies, Bird by Bird, Stitches,* etc.

"*Choosing Gentleness* - Let the wisdom within surround all the parts of you with uncommonly supportive love. It is not a normal book, which is a gift to us all."

SARK, bestselling author/artist, *Succulent Wild Woman, Eat Mangoes Naked,* etc., Creativity Mentor

"Our society is a supersaturated solution of experts, books and YouTube videos claiming to help you feel better about yourself and navigate your way through the labyrinth of thoughts, feelings and sensations that make up anyone's life.

What distinguishes Robyn's beautiful new book, *Choosing Gentleness,* from the rest of the pack is her ability to weave self-compassion into lives that have been inundated with unhelpful societal tropes."

Nicole S. Urdang, M.S, NCC, DHM, LMHC, Holistic Psychotherapist, Buffalo, N.Y.

"This is a delicious book full of bite size nuggets of wisdom on how to be kind to yourself."

Caitlin E. Matthews, D.C. Chiropractor, Ojai, CA

"*Choosing Gentleness* is a gift, literally and figuratively. Feeling given to by its wisdom and artistry, you will want to gift this book to everyone you know. Its essays, poems and drawings persuasively whisper that gentleness is the needed foundation for self-awareness and transformation. As you gently, patiently coax the characters of your internal world to share their feelings and concerns with you as their ever-developing compassionate witness, deep self-acceptance melts long held patterns. With that, new strength and growth appear. Counter-cultural! Revolutionary! Effective! Yes! And, truly, a great pleasure."

Carol H. Munter, co-author *Overcoming Overeating* and *When Women Stop Hating Their Bodies*

"*Choosing Gentleness* holds the concentrated wisdom of decades of healing and helping others heal, distilled into profound heart-easing medicine for those of us harmed by toxic mothering and our crazy-making patriarchal world."

Sonia Connolly, author of *Wellspring of Compassion* and *Presence After Trauma*

Tenderly Embracing
All the Ways that I Feel and Am:

Journaling to

Kindle Gentleness and Compassion

for Our Precious Selves

Robyn L. Posin
in collaboration with Barbara Fosbrink

Compassionate Ink
Box 725
Ojai, CA 93024

Compassionate Ink
Box 725
Ojai, CA 93024

Copyright ©2013 by Robyn L. Posin, Ph.D./Compassionate Ink

All rights reserved. Published in the United States of America. No part of this book may be used or reproduced in any manner whatsoever without written permission from the publisher except in the case of brief quotations embodied in critical articles or reviews. For information contact Robyn L. Posin, Compassionate Ink, Box 725, Ojai, CA 93024.

Cover Photo and Cover Design by Steve Rossman

Conceptualization and Design by Barbara Fosbrink with Robyn L. Posin

Author Photo by Barbara Fosbrink

Publisher's Cataloging-in-Publication data

Posin, Robyn L.
    Tenderly embracing all the ways that I feel and am : journaling to kindle gentleness and compassion for our precious selves / Robyn L. Posin ; in collaboration with Barbara Fosbrink.
        p. cm.
        ISBN 978-0-9891394-3-4

1. Self-actualization (Psychology). 2. Diaries --Authorship. 3. Diaries --Therapeutic use. 4. Self-realization. I. Fosbrink, Barbara. II. Title.

BF637.S4 .P669 2013
158.1 --dc23   2013919140

PRINTED IN THE UNITED STATES OF AMERICA

In Memory of

Zangwill Posin
(1916 – 2009)
My kind, gentle, deeply caring dad
whose tender, unconditional loving
helped me to save my life.

Lydia Gail Posin
(1948 – 2010)
My warm, compassionate, smart, beautiful, outrageously funny sister
who died too soon and before
she could heal into loving her precious self.

FOR THE GRANDMOTHERS:

The multi-racial, multi-ethnic, zany and

outrageous band of ancient spirit beings

that guide, nudge, whisper in my heart and protect me

as they gift me with words and images along the way of my journey

and welcome me into their circle.

*The women are called by an aching,
a yearning, a longing in their deeps.*

*It pulls at them in the middle of their ordinary lives like the pull
of the blood in the womb before it spills.*

A blind reaching of the heart leads them to the gathering place.

*They come as sleepwalkers and dreamers, deepening
as they move from their ordinary lives to the sacred ground.*

*The flow of their bodies, their hearts, their spirits, their knowing
is opening to the Mother's call to serve.*

*We are birthing ourselves into the womb circle
we are birthing to hold and nurture and
birth us back to Mother-sourcing power,*

*We feed the womb we are creating
To birth our new selves.*

- Robyn L. Posin

ACKNOWLEDGMENTS

The words and images that frame these pages have been gifts brought to and through me by the Grandmothers. Each year, since Winter Solstice 1984-New Year's 1985, the Grandmothers have whispered in my heart bringing – unbidden – an annual image and message (some years more than one) to be used for a greeting card I would then send to friends, family, clients and those former clients who've kept in touch with me. I've never counted on this magic, yet it continues year by year, sometimes arriving as early as May but always by December. My gratitude to these incredible spirit helpers is boundless. What they bring to me transforms my life and touches the lives of so many others, bringing us all reminders of the truths so often drowned out by the noise of our too-busy, too-feelings-phobic world.

One of the most miraculous gifts the Grandmothers have brought me is my dear friend Barbara Fosbrink, without whom neither this book nor the earlier, *Going Only as Fast as Your Slowest Part Feels Safe to Go: Tales to Kindle Gentleness and Compassion for Our Exhausted Selves* would have come to be. When we first met over twenty years ago, Barbara told me that she understood that we had work to do together. Since I had always done everything on my own and couldn't begin to envision collaborating with anyone, I dismissed her intuition. I was so wrong!

Barbara brings to our shared adventures a creative capacity for seeing the larger context of anything to which she turns her attention. She brings, as well, a commitment/devotion to and talent for collaboration along with a dedication to sharing her vision in ways that inspire and encourage one to re-envision the scope both of whatever the enterprise may be and of one's role in it. That she is (as am I) attuned to and acknowledging of the presence of Spirit/the Grandmothers is part of the blessing of her presence in my life.

On her own and, we both acknowledge, at the behest of the Grandmothers, Barbara has nudged and mentored me (sometimes crabbily kicking and screaming) into the twenty-first century. Because of her and with her help, I actually became computer-literate enough to build the first forthelittleonesinside.com website and the rest is our history.

This part of our adventure catalyzed one afternoon in 1998 as we sat in sacred space together having, as was our practice, called the Grandmothers to sit with us. Barbara was trying to help me see what she saw: I had a body-of-work that, were we to create a website, might be shared with a wider world. We sat on my studio floor surrounded by bits and pieces (she'd coaxed me to begrudgingly pull from various nooks and crannies in my cottage) of the essays and images I had intermittently been creating since the

1980s. I crankily resisted her vision while she gently persisted. Then, there was a magical moment when something cracked open. Quite suddenly, I saw the collection of papers through her eyes. Inspired, I began excitedly sorting all the pieces into four categories that ultimately became pathways for the website-to-be-born.

The only explanation we have for that discontinuous moment of illumination was that the Grandmothers were intent on moving us forward on the path we've travelled since then. That moment opened the door to creating a website the emergence of which opened the door to several years of me writing almost monthly tales for that site. The existence of the tales opened the way for me to begin gathering them (and other earlier stories we'd added to the website) into a manuscript in 2005. With Barbara cheerleading and offering feedback, after several more years of fits and starts, a revised version of that manuscript finally went to publication (in February 2013) as *Going Only as Fast as Your Slowest Part Feels Safe to Go: Tales to Kindle Gentleness and Compassion for Our Exhausted Selves.*

In the process of putting that first book together, the Grandmothers made it clear to us that the words and images from the annual greeting/note cards were to be saved for a companion journaling volume. Surrounding the otherwise blank pages of this journal book now in your hands, you'll find those words and images as well as fragments from song-chants (that also came from the Grandmothers) and seed thoughts/things to consider taken from the tales in the earlier book.

Tenderly Embracing All the Ways that I Feel and Am: Journaling to Kindle Gentleness and Compassion for Our Precious Selves is a milestone. Allowing Barbara to serve as the doorway through which the Grandmothers brought the design of this book has been a major step in my journey into creative collaboration. In the process, and despite my more narrow conception of my self, I've learned not only that I can collaborate creatively but, as well, that I actually love the process. For all this, I'm profoundly grateful.

Steve Rossman, (www.steverossman.com) dear cousin and photographer extraordinaire, six years ago took a snapshot of my altar that I immediately knew would be on the cover of the book yet to be born. Making that grab-shot work for the cover he designed for my first book involved him in tons of tinkering and a result that was, by his standards, less than perfect. In designing the cover for this book, Steve – with my blessings – took my altar to his studio so he could shoot a photograph that would better reveal Grandmother Namina in all her glorious exuberance. We agree that this one's perfect.

Shelley Buonaiuto (www.alittlecompany.net) created the marvelous sculpture, Grandmother Nanima, which sits on my altar in Steve's photo. Shelley graciously gave me permission to use the photo of Nanima for my book covers and promotional materials. Her amazing laughing grandmother sculptures are uncanny manifestations of the Grandmothers who live in my heart and to whom this book is dedicated.

Special thanks to Vivian Sudhalter (vivians09@att.net), professional wordsmith, for her eagle-eyed line editing and for her hilarious New York sense of humor.

AN INVITATION
TO BEING MORE TENDER AND LOVING
WITH YOUR PRECIOUS SELF

Throughout *Tenderly Embracing All the Ways that I Feel and Am: Journaling to Kindle Gentleness and Compassion for Our Precious Selves* you'll find words and images that invite you to dive deeply into your self as you journal. They provide inspiration for you to explore the many different and, perhaps, cut off or suppressed aspects of your self that constitute what might be called your inner family. They encourage you to explore the various voices that either keep a running background commentary going in your head or else languish unattended by you. As you engage in journal dialog with (perhaps even name) these parts of your self, you can begin to bring to consciousness the processes that usually direct (without your awareness) the quality of your self-talk, the ways you treat your self.

Hearing Our Inside Voices

Journaling-in-depth allows us the opportunity to listen to our untended parts, to begin to nourish them, to help them feel their ways through their feelings. Journaling-in-depth allows us to bring into awareness the often less than conscious shaping influences from societal, cultural and familial messages, to begin to challenge their truths and their relevance to our lives. Journaling-in-depth allows us to begin separating our authentic inner voice from the internalized chorus of these external messages.

The Impact of Outside Voices

We are all, to some greater or lesser degree, affected by living in a crazy-making, too-busy, out-of-balance world where the cultural trance of more, bigger, faster, do-it-yesterday sets the bar for what makes us feel worthy. Media images of success and beauty bombard us daily, liminally and subliminally, with idealized and photoshopped standards against which we are encouraged to measure ourselves. Inevitably, our merely human selves fall short of these impossible standards. It's a world that is feelings-phobic, particularly averse to any emotions of the so-called dark or shadow sort (namely, anything other than joy or bliss.) Is it any wonder that even those of us fortunate enough to have had fairly positive parenting in our families of origin frequently find ourselves dealing with the sense that we're either not enough or too much to be considered worthwhile or lovable.

We may hide our sadness or depression in order not to be seen as a "downer," a pariah. We may feel ashamed or guilty about the slightest bit of anger or rage – it's so not what nice girls should feel or else it's so "unevolved." And, particularly poisonously, some currently popular New Age flap would have us believe that letting ourselves feel any so-called negative emotions will only attract more of the same. Therefore, this framing insists, we should avoid such at all costs. Never mind that stuffing them can wreak havoc in our bodies and psyches!

The Impact of Our Family of Origin

In addition to these external societal and cultural pressures, many of us were raised in dysfunctional families by damaged caregivers. These caregivers had little or no patience, room or permission for us to be allowed to cry ("You better stop that crying before I give you something to cry about!") or to be cranky, have a tantrum or an angry outburst ("You go to your room, young lady, until you can act civilly!").

We have rarely gotten to experience the truth about feelings. Namely, that they are the energy of life, neither good nor bad in themselves, meant to be felt and expressed (safely). That all feelings, when allowed, have a natural trajectory: they build to a crescendo and then diminish and fall away.

Those of us raised by damaged caregivers – who often had little tolerance for the normal neediness of their children – learned very early to do without support and to believe that any needfulness was shameful. To be safe, we cut off from, suppressed or abandoned these needy, upset, sad or angry parts of our selves; unattended, they live on hidden away inside of us.

The Consequences of These Influences

All these pressures and prohibitions get internalized, becoming a less than conscious template for acceptable behavior; an internalization of myriad external voices becomes a chorus drowning out our own authentic inner realities. We lose any sense of our center. When we step out of line, these internalized voices harangue us to make sure we shape up so that we'll be safe from external retribution. These critical voices, meaning to protect us, are themselves often painfully harsh and punitive.

This journal workbook – with its seed-thoughts and threads to contemplate as you listen deeply inward and explore your own inner-knowing self – is meant to provide pathways to help you to transform these undermining influences and to build loving, gentle support for the truths of your own inner knowing.

Moving into Journaling

Arranging a space that feels private – one that can be kept free (for brief periods) from everyday human and technological distractions/interruptions – is essential to dropping into one's inner world. You might consider intentionally creating a sacred space to which you can come to explore your precious self as you use this book. It can help to have a simple ritual to mark the move from ordinary life into this special journaling time.

Lighting a candle, burning some incense or sage, or simply washing your hands while focusing your intention to come more deeply into your self are some possible transitioning rituals. Having colored markers or colored brush pens available to use for writing or drawing in these pages, possibly using your non-dominant hand, can open the way for the needs and feelings of long-neglected parts of your self to make themselves known to you.

As you go inward, you may begin to hear from your own inner guides, from however Spirit lives within you. You, too, may be reminded, as Robyn has been, of what is truly so for all of us on this journey:

We are all worthy, all lovable just for being – we do not need to earn love; love is grace, ours simply for breathing. Our first responsibility to all beings on the planet is to take the very best care of our own selves. The thing to do with feelings is to make it safe to feel all of them. Rest is a sacred act: as urgent, significant, honorable, productive and meaningful as any other purposeful act. Treating our selves with kindness and compassion is essential to life, growth and the capacity to be present in the world as a caring being.

Remember to go slowly with your self as you move into new inner territory. And, consider being as gentle and loving with you as you would be with anyone you truly cared about.

We hope that the snippets and seed thoughts you find in these pages may help you to begin (or enhance) your own explorations of how you might come to see and hold your precious self – all the ways you feel and all the ways you are – with more consistent generosity and gentle caring.

May your meanderings on and through these pages bring you:

An ever-increasing awareness of who and how you truly are,
An ever-expanding capability to compassionately embrace all of who you are,
An ever-blossoming ability to live from your deepest truths,
An ever-burgeoning capacity to give and receive love,
And, an ever-growing facility for experiencing delight and contentment with all the ways you are.

With warmest blessings for your journeying.

Robyn L. Posin
Barbara Fosbrink
Ojai, CA
Fall 2013

The journaling journey begins...

Consider giving your self permission to take exquisitely loving care of your very own self.

Slip the traces of containment. Loose the fetters of constraint. Dissolve the boxes that constrict.

Celebrate your radiance. Consecrate your confusion. Embrace your disowned shadow places.

Practice living fully in the middle of your beautiful, magical, still-evolving, sometimes lost, not always shining, all-of-who-you-are-right-now self.

Feeling vibrantly full-of-ourselves — miraculous, imperfect works-in-progress that we are — is everyone's birthright!

Consider the possibility of resting
whenever you're tired (what a concept)
and consider celebrating
your courageous self whenever you do.

Cherishing all the parts of myself with tender, gentle kindness . . .

I feed that which hungers within me.

Claiming not-knowing times as honorable,
empowering seasons of germinating
and inner preparation seems essential
to living more compassionately with our selves
and other beings.

Consider tenderly reassuring the parts of you
who are fearful of embracing not-knowing times,
of not-having-all-the-answers-right-now.

Our beings move always in the direction of growth. Ever evolving, the seeds of our next steps germinate in our deeps — even when the process is invisible.

Consider tenderly allowing your self
to go more slowly in any circumstances
in which you feel scared or anxious.

We honor the deepest truth: it is in moving through the shadow places that a path to our most radiant, reliable light is revealed.

Consider listening more attentively and carefully
to your body and belly feelings.

I honor and embrace my own vulnerability.

Moving only as fast as the slowest part of me feels safe to go,

Whenever you feel overwhelmed and unable to
slow the process of change
to a more manageable pace,

Consider living in the thinnest slice of now
that you can define.

When others' or our own critical voices label emotions negative or bad-for-us, the self-nurturer inside of us practices embracing our challenging feelings with ever greater tenderness and compassion.

Consider the practice of being patient and generous with your self in the feeling stuck times.

If we were to come to each moment,
to each other, always
not-wanting/not feeling wanted-from

What magic could happen here
in this so very between place.

Opening to the biggest space
of what wants to come through us,

Opening to the deepest yearning —
the unformed energy, the only-tending.

Choosing not to focus narrowly.
Choosing not to seek something particular.
Choosing not to go-looking for anything.

Floating, drifting
in not-wanting/not feeling wanted-from,

Still,
available,
ready to be moved
by Spirit and Soul.

Consider being tenderly patient
with and embracing of your vulnerable self
in the coming apart times.

This part's a dancer. Here's the dreamer so shy.

All of them needing my heart, ear and eye.

Consider being more tender, protective and attentive to the frightened parts of you.

Help me learn my self to praise.

When life gets hard,
remember how important it is
to lovingly remind your self that
it really is okay to be different.

Gently pruning away the dense tangle
Of constraint, should and expectation,
We open our own heart
To the nourishing flow of Spirit, unobstructed.

The endless lesson repeats:
Letting go, letting flow.

Consider how courageous and brave you are
to be engaged in this revolutionary process
of growing, healing and nourishing your self.

Where the sun's light illuminates the edge of darkness, rainbows are born.

Consider exploring how life feels and unfolds
when you frame broad open-ended intentions
instead of investing in detailed goals,
highly specific affirmations and
very carefully articulated visualizations.

Where the loving light of our own compassion illuminates the darkness within, healing, wholeness and peace are born.

Consider tenderly making safe space
to feel whatever you're feeling.

Rest, my fierce and weary one,

gentle sweet my babe. I am here enfolding you. You are truly safe.

Consider treating your self
with exquisite tenderness and acceptance.

In the sacred act of resting . . . I nourish my deepest self.

Consider spending some time turning
the light of your finely tuned sensitivity
toward your very own self.

Then, practice taking
the very best care of your very own self.

It's the greatest gift you can give
to all beings on this planet.

Sacred Mother calls me, singing in my heart. Asking me to cherish all of which I am a part.

When you feel discouraged about your progress, consider acknowledging the micro-steps you've actually taken while reminding your self that there is always further yet to go.

Remember, too, to be loving and comforting to your inner little one.

And, consider lovingly holding your own little one's hand as you grow.

Come and sit here beside me sweet little one.

I will hold you and rock you and sing to your heart.

Consider holding your empowered self
gently and with great care.

In the silence of the night, I'll be there to hold you tight.
In the places so alone, I'll be there to be your home.
In the places where there's pain,
You'll not be alone again.

Travel gently
as you begin to give your self
the love you've been hungering for.

With gentle loving kindness, I feed my very soul.

And, as I feed my own self, so I feed the whole.

Remember to lovingly remind your self
that you're always doing
the best you can in this moment.

Consider being loving and tender
with your in-this-moment self.

Hear your laughter. Hear your roar. Taste your tears and feel your fears.

Consider exploring and claiming
the fullness of your vulnerable, feeling self.

Help me to be fierce.

Consider using your
open or secret judgments of others
as opportunities to lovingly reclaim,
acknowledge and embrace
previously disowned parts of your self.

I am magical!

I am beautiful! I am wonderful! I am a miracle unto me!

Let your self notice whenever
you are openly or secretly judging
or feeling superior to anyone else
about some difference in your ways.
See if you can find more space for it to be okay
just to be you where and how you are.
And, do consider not judging your judging.

Consider being really loving with your self just
exactly where and how you are.

I listen and witness and lovingly hold,

delightedly watch the parts of me become exceedingly bold!.

Giving up the struggle of resisting the inevitable
(rather than giving up our feelings about it)
is what enables us to use our energies
to harvest the gifts hiding
in the middle of what feels so awful.

Consider lovingly honoring
your willingness to surrender your resistance
without surrendering your feelings.

In anger, I've hardened my heart.

When you feel uneasy, unsafe or not-okay
in any situation, consider taking your
apprehensions seriously
(no matter where they may be coming from)
and honoring them
by practicing such radical self-care.

In anguish, I've held on so tight.

Consider listening to your angry, mean-spirited or
nasty thoughts and feelings
as messages from deep within
about what's going on that's not okay for you.

In the between times,
when we're no longer
who we've been
and not yet
who we are becoming,
we practice letting go
of expectations,
timetables,
judgments.

Instead,
patiently and
with compassion,
we gently hold
our vulnerable,
in-transition selves,

Trusting
our organic
unfolding
to birth us
into that next place
at just the right moment.

Remember to be especially tender and
compassionate with your fallible,
mistake-making, simply human self.

In disappointment,

I've closed my heart.

Consider being gently respectful and loving
with the fearful parts of your self.

In soft whisperings from the heart,
the child-within offers you always the thread of your truth.

May you cherish that child, trust that voice and weave that thread
richly into the fabric of your days.

Consider bringing your own loving patience and attention to your own hungry or wounded parts.

For it's inward I travel, a journey rich and so sweet. And all of the magic I find here is me!

Consider taking time to be with and release
the energy of your anger in ways that feel safe.

Listen, listen, listen to your heart.

Consider taking some time
for pulling the covers over your head,
curling up with a teddy bear
and feeling sorry for your self the next time
you're having a hard time.

Listen, listen, listen to her fear.

Each time we can break the cultural taboos
against taking our emotions seriously by choosing
to respect our right to have them
or by allowing our selves to feel them
for as long as we feel them,
we are reclaiming more of our natural wholeness.

Remember to be kind and compassionate
with your self as you practice making space
to feel your feelings.

Listen, listen, listen to her tears.

Consider talking tenderly and gently to your self
as much of the time as you possibly can.

Little one, my sweetest one, my precious one, my own.
Come sit with me, come share with me.
Come let your self be known.

Consider the possibility that what you usually call
procrastination is really the sign
of a deeper, wiser part of your self
taking good care of you.

And, consider being really loving and gentle
with that part of your self.

Cherished one, oh treasured one, I'm awfully glad you're here.

Little one, my sweetest one, my precious one, my dear.

Consider being tender and careful with your self
as you explore the gentle magic of slowing down.

Help me hold my self as I grow, get ready to know:

angers and rages, griefs, fears and more that are locked deep inside me from so long before.

Consider being really tender with
and attentive to your super-achieving,
rest-starved self.

Gather armfuls of silence. Fill baskets with stillness.
Weave a cocoon of gentle quiet, a comforting bower of solitude in which to rest and be reborn.

Consider slowing down and listening in
to the deep knowing place within you
whenever you're tempted to rush through
something that seems too hard to feel.

Allowing the love of The Great Mother to enfold me,

I remember to more lovingly mother and cherish my self.

Consider giving your self (or receiving)
the gift of empty, still time to rest and
replenish your cherished self.

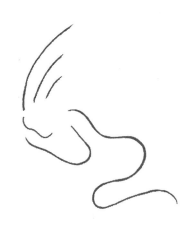

Practicing tenderness, kindness and forgiveness toward our selves, we blossom.

Blossoming, we re-create the garden: a gentler, more loving world.

Remember to be very gentle with your self
as you practice moving away from busyness.

Cultivate the courage to embrace whatever is unfolding in your life and whatever cranky, hating feelings you may have about it. Hold your precious self with tender compassion as you go.

Consider loving and accepting
your self no matter what anyone else
(or your own inner critical voice)
thinks or says about you.

Remember always:

every moment is sacred, every task a teaching, everything we embrace transforms us.

Consider being
as tender as you possibly can be
with your wounded, upset, hurt or angry self.

Knowing that sharing from our deepest core serves us much better than all that's gone before.

Consider honoring the rightness for you
of your very own path and your very own pace.

Delighting in all the baby steps along the way of my journey . . . I celebrate the wonder of my unfolding.

Consider being incredibly
gentle with your self.

It does not matter whether how we are in the moment is born from our woundings or from

our wholeness. What matters is how lovingly, compassionately and unconditionally we can embrace how we are in the moment.

With this embracing and dedication we create

the fertile inner soil that nourishes our continued blossoming and unfolding.

Consider treating your self with gentleness
and compassion in the dark feelings times.

Every step on the road is my coming home.

Every breath on the road is my coming home. Spirit is calling, my heart will be free. For I'm coming home, and home is me.

Consider giving your self permission
to be just exactly where you are
while you're there —
even when you truly wish you didn't have
to be there at all.

Our world, life swirling
Turbulent, out of control
At the edge of the abyss.
Emotional white water
Overwhelm:
Feeling helpless,
Powerless, anguished
Awash in fearful frustration,
Despair.

No resistance possible.
Breathing deeply,
Yielding to the vortex
Howling in rage, terror, grief.

Surrender takes us deeper:
Through the center
To our center.
In exhausted stillness
Knowing is reborn,
Direction revealed.

In the turbulent times
Try living
In the thinnest slice of now
That you can define.
And, remember
To practice being
Extravagantly gentle
With your very
Precious self.

Consider listening inward
to your belly-feelings when you feel confused or
any other time you remember that
they're a source of knowing
that is constantly available to you.

I promise to stay near, and help her be safe, so she'll grow and she'll blossom and take up her space.

Consider being more loving,
generous and compassionate
with your delicate, less than perfect self.

Deep in my heart sings a voice.

it whispers to me of the choice to slow down, soften, let go.

Consider exploring the possibility of
giving your self permission to stop (or not to start)
doing things that feel like too much work.

True selflessness and compassion flow not so much from transcending as from abundantly loving the self.

May you give your self (and all the rest of the beings on our planet) the gift of loving your self more clearly and generously in the days ahead.

May you consider exploring the practice of
spending small bits of time alone,
treating your self lovingly.

May you consider honoring that practice
if you're already doing it.

And, may you remember to be tender with your
dear and precious self.

We'll laugh and we'll sing and we'll dance and we'll run, through streams and through meadows, all dappled in sun.

Consider letting your self just be exactly
as you are, right now —
as if it's okay with you to be
your very own unfinished
work-in-progress self.

Welcoming our sorrow, anger, fear, despair, jealousy and hate as openheartedly as we do our joy, delight, excitement, elation and love, allows these intense feelings room to swell, crest, reveal their teachings & naturally fade away.

This always moves us forward.

Remember to be as compassionate
as possible with your fearful selves.

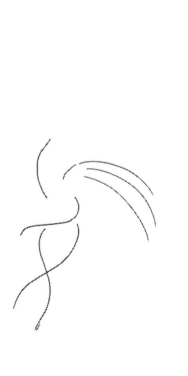

Change moving quickly.
Everything intense
Overflowing, too muchness.
Then, remembering:
Close eyes, breathe
Deeply, slowly
Again, and again
And again.
Feeling the slowing
In our body
Calling us lovingly
Into the very thinnest
Slice of now,
Into just-this-moment,
Here, where always
We have all we need
To balance
To cope
To hold ourselves
Safe.
Remembering:
Close eyes, breathe
Deeply, slowly
Again, and again
And again.

Remember to be really gentle with your self, not
to ask your self
to move ahead into anything
that you're not ready for
and not to harass your self
for taking all the time you need
to become ready.

Our daily practice: cultivating compassion toward our selves, tenderly embracing all these ways that we are. Waking from the delusion: perfection is grossly over-rated.

Consider treasuring your dear and quirky selves.

We'll talk and we'll dream and we'll plan and we'll scheme, snuggle and nuzzle, giggle and scream.

Imagine the possibilities in bringing your
unconditional loving to your own self.

Dancing at the edge is a delicate dance of balance. Of merging and

emerging in the "no-place" between words and images, between silence and sound, between what is dying away and what is coming to be.

Consider hearing judgmental comments about
your behavior as messages telling you something
significant about the judging person
rather than as conveying any truth about you.

And, consider practicing letting your self
just be exactly who and as you are.

What is at the edge is always the beginning of new directions.

Next time you find your self talking
meanly to your self, consider the possibility
of listening deeper to hear who else inside of you
might be trying to get your attention.

If you can hear that scared self,
consider the possibility
of helping her feel more safe.

And, consider treating that scared part
with great tenderness.

There is no "right" way, only the way that we choose.

There is no "right" time, only that which feels timely. There are no "consequences," only the way things evolve.

If you don't feel ready yet for an opportunity
that presents itself, consider letting it pass
and trusting there will always be
other more-right-for-you
openings down the road.

No need for vigilance or pushing. These only disrupt the organic flow of our unfolding.

Instead, we learn to practice gentleness and patient allowing, remembering to trust that growth and change are our true nature.

Consider remembering to approach all that you
do and all the ways that you are
with curiosity: interest in how you are wired;
see how much more gentle you become
with your self and watch how you thrive.

Dear Mother of All, come take my hand, while I am frightened alone to stand. Wrap your love around my heart while I mend my broken parts.

Remember that beginnings
are also times of endings, that beginnings
are times for both celebration and grieving —

Consider giving your self permission to feel
all the seemingly contradictory feelings.

From the core,
Energy rising.
Vibrating.
Burgeoning forth.
Stretching us.
Cracking us open.
Unfurling wings
We did not know we'd had.
Lifted on gusts of joy,
We are soaring
Beyond the furthest reaches
Of any self we have known.

May you find the courage to go only as fast as
the slowest part of you feels safe to go.

All of us worthy, precious beings deserving love just exactly as we are

this very moment: flawed, ragged, often bumbling works-in-progress.

THE HEALING JOURNEY

In each of us, often deeply buried and inaccessible, lives a vibrant, inviolable creature self – the pure essence of who we truly are. This deep self, our wise and knowing simple animal being – when not interfered with – unerringly, instinctively moves us toward that which grows and nurtures us. Just as unfailingly, it moves us away from all that endangers us on any level.

The whole process of socialization in our modern western culture is a relentless curriculum that surrounds and embeds us in values, prescriptions and social forms that undermine, contradict and deny the credibility of these inner urgings.

So much of what ails us and causes us much intense grief and struggle in our lives comes primarily from our being cut off/alienated from the knowings of this essential self. The pain of this alienation is further compounded by the endless liminal and subliminal messages that threaten us with the loss of the love, care and connection with all who matter to us should we choose to turn inward to make connection with our deep self a priority. We are warned that self-ishness is always unacceptable and reprehensible.

We have come to be frightened of authenticity, of strong emotions of any sort: joy, sorrow, anger, grief, fullness-of-self. We have learned to fear and override the need for slowness, the need for rest: for empty time, space to be still and quiet, inward, reflective.

The healing, coming home process is one of unlayering: of shedding and separating ourselves from the misguided conventions, beliefs and requirements by which society has disconnected us from the place of wholeness within us. It is the slow, careful process of uncovering and exploring the depths of who we truly are.

Gently and lovingly we create a safe oasis in which first to observe and then to begin suspending the self-undermining ways we have been taught to live. In this oasis, away from the clamor of things as they are, we allow the truth within us to surface, to be heard. Over time and with great care and patience, we begin the practice of living from the center of ourselves, our truths.

SOME LOVING REMINDERS FOR THE PRACTICE

The loving acceptance you so deeply hunger for can never reach you
until you've learned to give that gift to your self.

You are entitled to love your self just exactly as you are right now.

You are always doing the best you can in this moment. If you could
do better, you would do better.

Practice being as gentle with your self as you would be with anyone else
you truly cared about.

Listen in to your body and your belly feelings, they will always tell
you what's so for you.

Practice making room and safe space to feel all of your feelings.

Speak kindly and lovingly to your self as much of the time as possible.

When you feel sad, depressed or in grief, take time and space to fold inward to be
with the aching and the tears until they're done. (They will be done, sometime.)

Listen to your angry, nasty, mean-spirited feelings – they tell you when something
not-good-for-you is going on.

When you feel scared or anxious, move more slowly; ask the frightened part what it would need
in order to feel safe.

Go only as fast as the slowest part of you feels safe to go.

Remember that growth is a process, not an achievement. When you feel discouraged, take time to
lovingly acknowledge how far you've already come...there is always further yet to go.

Remember, too, that all life moves in cycles...what has been must
often come apart before what is to be can come together.

When you're tired, rest, especially when there's no-time-to-rest.

Remember that rest is a sacred act – as significant, meaningful, productive and honorable
as any other purposeful act.

When it gets hard, remind your self that it's okay to be different.

Applaud all the baby steps along the way of your journey.

Acknowledge the wonder of your persistence in the difficult times.

Marvel at the miracle of your courage and your trust-in-the-process.

Delight in your self at every possible opportunity:
You are a magnificent work-in-progress.

ABOUT THE AUTHOR

Robyn spent her first 32 years as a hyper-self-critical super-achiever never at peace with her self. Just past her 32nd birthday, at the urging of a voice deep within her, she dropped out of that life, took to the road in a self-contained van and began the journey of uncovering who she might be without the overlay of all her driven excelling.

Her journaling with words, drawing and collaging – a significant part of that process – continues to be a way she explores and stays in touch with the many voices deep inside her. The words and images in this book have taken shape in her ongoing journals.

Now in her early 70s, she lives life in the slow lane, at peace (at last) with all the ways she is and isn't. With two affectionate, quirky kitties in a small rented cottage surrounded by a private meadow, she grows food and flowers in containers, feeds myriad seed-feeding and humming-birds, spends endless hours reading in her hammock, floating in her hot tub, puttering around the house and garden, walking about town and on the local trails, working with clients a few hours every other week, occasionally hosting women's wisdom circles, writing almost-monthly blogs for her websites and sleeping in a windowed tent in her meadow year round except for rainy or windy days.

Writing and making art weave randomly through her days. *Go Only as Fast as Your Slowest Part Feels Safe to Go: Tales to Kindle Gentleness and Compassion for Our Exhausted Selves* (her first book) – birthed in a seven-year process of going only as fast as **her** slowest part felt safe to go – was published in February 2013. This journal is intended as a companion to *Go Only...*, providing space to further explore whatever was stirred in you by the themes and possibilities raised in that earlier book.

Should your explorations in these journal pages lead you to consider consulting with a therapist who's traveled this road, Robyn is a California Licensed Psychologist who has been working with clients since 1964. She is available for open-ended, one-time or ongoing individual consultations by phone or in person in Ojai, California.

Her commitment is to creating safe space in which to help people (re)connect with and honor the wisdom of their own inner knowing: the wisdom that can guide us to living life more in harmony with who we truly are, even in this crazy-making, invalidating world.

If you'd like to talk about the possibility of arranging an individual consultation and check on her current fee, please drop her an email at Robyn@compassionateink.com.

ORDERING INFORMATION

Compassionate Ink is the publishing imprint through which Robyn offers her nourishing collection of resources celebrating going slowly, compassionately embracing all of our feelings, nurturing the Little Ones Inside and honoring the Sacred Feminine.

The forthelittleonesinside.com and the compassionateink.com websites host the words, images and tales Robyn has been creating over the years. These have all emerged from her dedicated life-long journey of healing (and helping others heal) from the harshness that our crazy-making world visits upon all of us, especially women. (Robyn L. Posin, Ph.D. is a licensed psychologist in private practice in Ojai, California.)

Go Only as Fast as Your Slowest Part Feels Safe to Go: Tales to Kindle Gentleness and Compassion for Our Exhausted Selves is also available in Kindle, iBook and Nook formats. After a first read of these emotionally uncensored, autobiographical healing tales, many open the book randomly in moments of unease, confusion or doubt and read the chapter to which they've opened as a message from Spirit/their Deep Self.

Tenderly Embracing All the Ways that I Feel and Am: Journaling to Kindle Gentleness and Compassion for Our Precious Selves is a natural extension of and companion to *Go Only as Fast as Your Slowest Part Feels Safe to Go*. A bound 8.5" x 11" journal, its otherwise blank pages are edged with words and images to inspire and invite you to kindle gentleness and compassion for your precious self as you write, draw, explore and reflect on your journey.

Choosing Gentleness: Opening Our Hearts to All the Ways We Feel and Are In Every Moment, is a collection of short essays and poems-with-drawings that encourage us to give our selves permission to be exactly how we are in every moment—to honor and embrace wherever we are in our process without criticism and to treat all of our feelings with tenderness and compassion.

Catalog of Treasures

Ordering information for the Remembering and Celebrations Cards, the deck of 64 bookmark-size cards that you've seen, paired with their tales, in *Go Only as Fast as Your Slowest Part Feels Safe to Go: Tales to Kindle Gentleness and Compassion for Our Exhausted Selves* can be found at www.compassionateink.com/catalog-of-treasuresalt. There you'll also find ordering information for Robyn's collection of healing note cards, postcards, poster cards and amulets.

FONTS USED

Many thanks to the artists whose fonts are used in Tenderly Embracing All the Ways That I Feel and Am: Journaling to Kindle Gentleness and Compassion For Our Precious Selves. They include:

FORUM

Title, Acknowledgements and Invitation by Denis Masharou

Of Wildflowers and Wings

Cover Title Font and Journal pages by Britney Murphy Design

Made in the USA
Columbia, SC
29 August 2020

17962743R10146